Busy Machines
Tractors

Written by Amy Johnson   Illustrated by Ela Smietanka

MILES
KELLY

Tractor power!

On the farm, tractors work busily with other machines to get jobs done.

Front loader

They TRUNDLE...

Baler

Hedge trimmer

and JUDDER...

Tractor

and CHUG.

Trailer

All about tractors

Tractors are very powerful! They are mainly used to pull other farm machines.

Steps to the cab

Huge tyres for driving across bumpy fields

The cab is high up so the driver can see all around

Mudguards stop earth flying everywhere

Different machines are joined to the back of the tractor.

Balers make hay, straw or grass into bales

Seed drills plant seeds

Ploughs turn the soil

The plough makes rows called furrows as it is pulled through the soil

Riding high

Tall crops need tall tractors! This **crop sprayer** has extra-big wheels so it can travel above plants like sunflowers.

Nozzles on the boom spray the crops to protect them from disease and help them grow

The sprayer's arm is called a boom

sowing seeds

The fields have been ploughed – now they're ready for planting.

Seed drills drop seeds into the ground in rows then cover them with soil.

Busy machines!

Find your favourite farm machine!

Super tractors!

Big Bud is the largest farm tractor in the world. It was built in the USA over 40 years ago. It has a super-powerful engine and huge tyres.

Tracked tractors have tough rubber tracks that don't squash the ground as much as wheels.

Harvesters are used in forests to fell trees. They have a long arm that bends and a claw-like grabbing tool.

Harvest time

Combine harvesters cut crops such as wheat and oats, and then separate the grains from the stalks.

Potatoes bounce along a conveyor belt on the potato harvester, out into a trailer.

Chute unloads into a trailer

Grass is blown into a chute

Forage harvesters are used to gather grass and corn for animal feed.

Cotton bale

Cotton harvesters pick fluffy white clumps of cotton from their plants.

All about balers

When a field is full of hay bales, it means a **baler** has been hard at work.

The baler is pulled by the tractor

2 Inside, the hay is squashed and bundled into shape by rollers

1 The baler picks up hay as it moves over it

Bales are collected by special bale-handler tractors. Some can lift six in one go!

3 The back opens and the finished bale rolls out

Lots of jobs

It takes many kinds of machines to keep a busy farm running.

I'm great for clearing straw, mud and muck!

Skid-steer loader

Trailer

Orchard tractor

Muck spreader

The boom slides out to reach high-up things

Boom lift

Pick-up truck

Utility tractor

Rotary mower

Tractor tours

On open days, visitors to the farm can go on tractor rides.

The **milk tanker** is being filled up.

It's feeding time! The **front loader** carries hay for the cows.

Some sheep are being loaded
onto the **animal trailer**.

From the **trailer**, visitors have
a great view of the farm.

The farmer is using an
all-terrain vehicle to
check on the pigs.

Combine team

When grain is ripe, it takes whole teams of combines to harvest big areas.

The crops need to be harvested quickly so less is wasted